T001043З

Hesitating Once to Feel Glory

HESITATING
ONCE TO FEEL
GLORY

MALEEA ACKER

NIGHTWOOD EDITIONS

2022

Nightwood Editions
P.O. Box 1779
Gibsons, BC VON 1V0
Canada
www.nightwoodeditions.com

COVER ART: Lacey Decker Hawthorne
COVER DESIGN: Christian Fink-Jensen
TYPOGRAPHY: Carleton Wilson

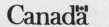 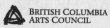

Canada Council   Conseil des Arts
for the Arts   du Canada

BRITISH COLUMBIA
ARTS COUNCIL

BRITISH
COLUMBIA

Nightwood Editions acknowledges the support of the Canada Council for the Arts, the
Government of Canada, and the Province of British Columbia through the BC Arts Council.

This book has been produced on 100% post-consumer recycled, ancient-forest-free paper,
processed chlorine-free and printed with vegetable-based dyes.

Printed and bound in Canada.

LIBRARY AND ARCHIVES CANADA CATALOGUING IN PUBLICATION

Title: Hesitating once to feel glory / Maleea Acker.
Names: Acker, Maleea, 1975- author.
Identifiers: Canadiana (print) 2022015130X | Canadiana (ebook) 20220151326 |
    ISBN 9780889714144 (softcover) | ISBN 9780889714151 (EPUB)
Subjects: LCGFT: Poetry.
Classification: LCC PS8601.C535 H47 2022 | DDC C811/.6—dc23

CONTENTS

TRIPE AND CAKE

The body is an animal
from which longing springs.

The hands, hermit crabs. The eyes,
moustached bus drivers. The forehead,

corrugated tin roof
over spangled Guadalajara girls.

I am a salt shaker of happiness.
My thirst knows this plastic table

like the back of your hand.
Why won't you sample the unachievable pleasure?

My shaker breaks loose and cartwheels the main street,
through the dust heaps, the potholes, the nicked

knuckles of the stoneworker. It settles
in a foundation crack. It ticks back and

forth in the evening's drum roll. It dries
and shims the leftover heat. It wants things.

It's almost three and dressed as a *pirata*.
It's eating tripe and cake.

It's not speaking because it can't
eat it and want it, too.

TACOS

The best part of the day is the night.
I go searching for tacos, unhappy
as I walk. The streets are empty
except for people piling firewood
for the holiday. I am the ghost that passes.
The road ends. I backtrack
through some trees
to the stone pathway. Ahead,
a highway materializes.
I turn the corner. A car dealership, a man
behind glass adding numbers
in a store full of fans. Then, a naked bulb
suspended above dirt,
smoke, plastic chairs. Hot dogs?
Tacos!
Radishes float like little wounded hearts.
I am a compass needle swinging
yes to everything.
It is important to hold
their greasy, hot circles properly.
Three, or better, two fingers. Approach
from the side. No one talks to me, but I manage not
to spill. The trucks waft past. The daughter
smiles at her father. I belong
somewhere, but then I am finished
am an unmatched sock again,
old love silent at the other end of the country.
The girl with braces, the staring father, the brother
wicks my plate of its plastic bag.

I am the doubtful guest.
So I get up and the plastic bag
rises into the air and follows me
like a silly translucent mule. It is the pale
little mule of quietness and
of the strangled look a man gives
to the air when presented
with the affection of a woman, a mule
with a wooden saddle, a mule loaded
to the traces with sorrow but
never, ever, no,
never with regret.

THE TRUMPET SPEAKS TO THE CROWD

I live behind a small farm
of roosters that speak as they like,
which is always,
and a donkey, some sheep
and a cow, or so say
my neighbours. None have seen her.
There are six cypress trees.
Five tilt their heads in unison, agreeing
with any judgment I pass.
The sixth is contrary and swears
no allegiance.
Joy impossible, then ever-present
as they get it together. Their heads
loll; it depends. It
depends which key I use.
One opens another prison.
One hangs at the throat
of a bull named Bodacious,
whose habit of knocking
rodeo kings in the head with his own
has allowed several surgeons
in El Paso to afford third homes.
Sense ships up the road again,
to a café where a trumpet
with a woman's vaudeville body
looks at the boy selling pies and
judges him without translation.
I could eat them all, she says,
and buys none. A little god

like a tsetse fly finds her ear. It wears
false eyebrows and a moustache. Two canals
diverge in a wood
and the fly takes the most sonorous,
stirs shrill to coronet, failure
as a philosophy that thrills
the folds, as though
in a darkened theatre
with one's heart pumping, hooked
to an unseen apparatus that
whisks blood to and
from a naked roof,
it had found the answer
to anything.

THE WHOLE FISH

I come from a long line of imaginaries.
Our lives are spent wasting like debarked dogs.

We save the best for the lost. Our beauty
legendary but off-putting.

We are not trustworthy. We don't
pull the grain in time. We clean the house

out and sell the treasures. We are the stick
marking drought, not the water's balm—

everything we touch, everyone we
think we love. So, Imaginary,

do you recognize me still?
Our letters down to three lines,

written in each other's countries.
Let's imagine our possible life:

one desk, two writers, one heart, two
languages, one landscape, two minds.

At dinner you eat the whole fish.
In the night a child with blackest

of humours grows an inch a day between us.
In light the woman you do not cheat with,

the man I do. A few rainstorms, a cough,
a kiss, some Coca-Cola field workers,

so much wind. Here are the eyes,
the bones, the fins. Can I go now?

Is this enough?

I didn't think so.

INTERIORS

I am trying to become an envelope
of nothing but dust; I fold
my edges so sharp

I score myself
trying to create an inside.
This is after the wedding, the sad

eighteen-year-olds three months gone,
not touching the whole ceremony.
She tried to smile, accepted

a tissue from her father. Marriage is
not a prison, he spoke, when asked.
Do you know where I am? I know

what you're feeling. I know you won't
say it. We could go on like this forever,
like the bus driver entangled in Nueve Calles

the neighbourhood's men trotting
to rescue. In a thirty-six-point turn
he fulcrums the corner. The briefest of waves

after he finds the straight and
grounds the pedal. It doesn't get better.
Fucking is nothing, but desire,

well, it's like a midnight clam dig
when deep down you feel
what you want

in the dark and the muck
only to have it take you in its mouth
and cleave you to the bone.

Sometimes I think we can see
the world before it began,
and that's what makes us
so sad. Before the world began

there were swallows flying
across a lakeside field
as the sun allowed the trees to shade it.
There were fallen leaves

from dry seasons that made
a golden road. And there was
silver and stone and clover,
and a man on horseback

with a dog with no tail
that loped across the field
in a lazy semi-crescent as though
drawing the orbit of a small moon.

There was a burro
on a ten-foot length of rope
stomping a dust patch in the earth.
And there were pelicans

with injured wings hand-fed
by a waiter and so many willows—
so many!—growing by the water's edge.
There was the clink of bottles

before the world began
and so its sound still
makes us melancholy
the way ice can, booming

on a river in spring
or tilling a glass in a woman's hand.
Stones, too, uncovered from earth
pockmarked with clam houses,

and also clams. Pianos, there were
pianos, too, their cascade made us
restless, they could not offer
more nuance than the half note.

Things kept coming
before the world began, and stacked
and tumbled over themselves
in drifts like snow,

insensible. The world
before the world was annotated,
expansive, all the stones
the boys could throw,

never hesitating once to feel
glory, to feel jealousy,
boredom, and the nostalgia
the grass feels as it clambers

above itself, and loses
its former lives in the clean,
disintegrating thatch
and dust and clay.

The sadness of the alternate-
armed rower, who walked his boat
to shore! The sadness of the far shore
and the thud of a foot against a ball,

the bent hook of wire hanging
from a tree's lost branch stub,
the question in the ibis' voice
the sudden flash of a red bird

like a compass of ink in the brush.
Before the world began
there were bells that never
rang the correct time, and wings

and spheres of sad eggs in water.
The burro walked his circle
and the carpenter never saw
his children further

than sixth grade. He never
painted his room yellow or cooked
on anything but a burner
on a board. And the neighbour,

after the party, she never
gave the plate back though
she said she would,
she always said she would.

FAVOURITE THINGS

One: the cypresses
bending in wind,

their tips super-
sensitive sea pens.

Two: the occasionally
marching marching band—

tubas saxophones trumpets
three blocks away—

sometimes lets its clarinet have the stage.
Noodles. A klezmer flourish

that breaks old stems into new
hummingbird into humming

and bright bird. Three:
the mind briefly at rest,

stones in its closet, the air-proof,
cauterized shell of stillness,

allowing breath.
Green wind,

green mountains,
jade air west to the sea.

THE DICTATOR

The Dictator puts on *Music for 18 Musicians*,
Section IV. These are the last hours
of the year, before Maximino
gives his children to the Americans.

They still live in two rooms
beside his carpenter's
workshop illuminated by stars
by night, by dusk by day.

Section V begins.
The ironworker has finished
his calla lily doors. He's doing
something pedestrian now, maybe

the framing for a toilet. The carpenters
drag their new saw inside, up
the furred cement stairs. In two rooms
two beds sleep five, on the roof

the cistern, the tree that hides
bathing, the neighbours from which
there is no invitation.
In an hour, the bats will emerge

from their little ceramic shells.
As the last of the sun stumbles
into the lake the Dictator,
parked at the edge with his extraordinary

car battery and his ridiculous heart,
turns up the speaker on the roof
and cues up some Lionel Richie,
then a little Brahms. It's early

Lionel Richie so it's okay.
Notice the stomped,
broad-leafed grass, the gelatine air
at its inconsequential hinge,

the last cloud bank spitting
out a star. Is it possible
he is playing out our life?
Baker, Sosa, Ibáñez, Bach,

pulled in all directions,
all incomputable, we are
little racing dogs just bathed.
Someone lights a bonfire

in the field of the Roma.
Maxi's children
fix themselves at the edge.
The oars of the fisherman

flake the mother-of-pearl lake
as the Dictator slides
on his black gloves, lifts
his wine from the car's

roof, pulls out all the stops.
Cities fall. He takes
a drink, they bubble up again
as the dust of the unremarkable

end meets its maker, the one
with the skin of damp gold,
his palm up, palm open as the mind
of a dog, as the tricks of a child.

APPROXIMATE A SINGULAR FEELING

The history of the Americas
could be illustrated by the bushes
I planted on the property of
my neighbour. He is due back this morning.

In the rising storm the rose branches return
to shadow puppets, but no one snickers
behind the screen. Reading right to left
I watch the giant sky picture change.

Here's the brief reprieve
from the undertaker's eye, O then
we will suffer. Meanwhile, on a Mexican soccer pitch
a teen playing a *torito* sets

to running. Shooting roman candles
out his ass, the stick-and-paper effigy
on fire around him, he's thinking
about kinds of kissing: the Moby Dick,

the Hygienist, the Panini.
I'll tear myself away from you
as one would leave a friend,
wrote Salomé. All I'm doing

is sitting in this room waiting
for the machinery of our heartbeats
to syncopate sometime
into a constancy like Claude glass.

There is not much to see.
A desk, a lamp on fire,
some dreaming pencils. Our hymn
to life is at the hinge of

an imaginary errand for oranges
and cheese. Our arms full,
it's either the beckoning of distant
shining things or the kitchen's damp.

We'll not reach either.
The kitchen of our impossibilities!
Together only for the hesitating
moment, the song wavers, we are marched,

separated back to what it knows. Ours
the miniscule pendulum
careening from kismet to the glorious
crying of the food in its plastic bags,

the noise of a thousand cities
a murmuring hush in our ear,
to be cut in two, to be turned inside out,
to be taken by you on any mid-morning.

HOVERCRAFT

The trouble with introspection
is it keeps changing its mind.
Most of the time I sit on a precipice

of memory built somewhat like
a camping mattress. The dust-mote floor
an inch away, the wires above blanketed

like a Cuban mezzanine; it's hard
to find a supportive position. Outside,
the lavender plant is frozen.

One of the drafty spaces
in my chest is in the shape of a dog,
and at least one, your hands

resting and waiting above a meal.
The mattress hovers me.
It is from the Realm of the Kings,

as is the glowing silver
barbecue on the deck and all
my sad little cooking implements

stolen away from warmer people.
I know you have this trouble, too.
It's like we're made of tablecloths

strategically printed to show
our failures as breezy ferns
and a wafting of trumpet flowers.

The streets below continue
their gentrifications and ablutions.
You're floating above me

like a crane fly, its rocket tail contracts
until the little Japanese bowl of its head
tilts a bucket of bare twigs

onto my chest, which has begun
to retreat into itself the way
a cloth's weave can hide a strand

inside its own skin.
If I can't be a thread anymore
I want to be a hole.

FEALTY OF THE SHORT, DARK FEELING

I've been experimenting with which additives
make the black crater inside myself
shrink or grow. The recipes amaze.

Loneliness fills it with potash.
A particularly tender person
burns the interior like a November pumpkin.

I'm like a porch dog on the top step
arrowed toward the world. Occasionally
I blunder down and make a half-hearted nest

in the grass. Mostly my interiors are clear-cuts
on some northwestern island southern people
think is perpetually covered in snow and

eastern people think is evidence
of our weakness. We're just a minority here,
amongst the brightening alder stems

and the occasional uncut fir standing
like a starved sheriff in the field. My west
is a peculiar mix of fermented berries

and machinery parts covered in moss
that makes the cogs shine like onyx,
which I have always wanted to put

in a poem cage and adorn like a Christmas
palm. I know I will never be good.
My worry machine is not the shape

of a country in the Americas. It does not purr
as the machete's blade rises. It is a soft
multiple feeling like being alone

on a lakeside walkway in the midst
of one hundred families, then returning weeks later
on someone's arm and not even recognizing

the place. A dog finds the entrance
to the crater, enters as through a
rabbit tunnel, her tail faintly swaying.

The invincibility of appearances
is where failure becomes universal,
becomes something even you are doing. It's where

the poem cage's front viewing window
opens to the public and everyone
can see the prey I eat wasn't caught by me.

COMING TO PIECES

That night he waited for me on the street and we drove to Chapala
in a 1980 Ford he borrowed from his father. You switch gears
by grasping the steering column in both hands and counting the clicks.
We walked the *malecón* and the docks where waves were breaking
against the fixed fingers and *lirio* washed against the shore
after its travels through Oaxaca dams, down river, into the ever-
shrinking lake. I could tell he felt afraid near water.
On a bench at the shore we drank tequila until
the plastic bottle was empty, then wandered without direction
in the gentle truck. At Tacos Moya we had five and I was
still hungry. We drove to Rincón, a small turn between villages
where the road grows dark and the wetland spills under cliffs
and crickets, pelicans and ibises stretch themselves into filigree.
Speaking and touching. At one point I thought I might be
breaking into blossom, but having learned to curb it
I pushed at his skin, which was like antler velvet.
It's *your* skin, he said. I gift it to you.
The west wind faded and bats flew over us.
We both had to work in the morning. When we talked
we faced outward and married one another's arms
and fingers and heads to one another's bodies, and it felt
like becoming a planet, out in the dark, with a fragrant light
tearing our lives into pieces where each met the others' edge.

THE DICTATOR BEFORE THE RAINY SEASON

Every few months about ten seconds
of natural happiness.
My head's brick oven lifts its top
and the new ceiling is just stars.

Then it's okay that I am
a painted table cracked and peeling
in a hut without a floor,
supporting torn coasters marked

with phone numbers by men
who want to take me
to the south side, show me
their horses in Wyoming. But

mostly it's my grandfather—
his batting hand and dizziness,
carless, his clubs in the corner,
his brown eyes turning

from the pages of the television
to the flickering elms, their
leaves dropping and re-manifesting—
that lives inside the black

crater that is my displacement
and my six p.m. euphoria. We all
live for something. The Dictator's
name is Antonio. When we met I

could feel the myth folding in on itself,
closing its own edges like
a chiton. The pieces locked and the thing
was gone and saved as we are gone

and saved when we touch another.
Sometimes he is in a field cooking meat
or playing a saxophone with headphones
and sometimes he parks his car

around the corner from my house
and blares Bebel Gilberto until
I come down with a drink.
It is four months since the last rain.

The hills on the far side of the lake
apologize. It's a murky territory of dust
when a person comes up to you,
takes you to his tiny, red-walled rooms,

offers orange juice, sets up
the battery-powered speakers.
Go ahead. Touch the mirage.
Tell him all the inconsequential facts:

the prize you almost won, the small
parade of ants that skirted, then
tracked your foot as the *gaviotas*
like white napkins stole away

from a black dog and the wind
brought the cardboard set down.
Unlicensed, a stretched cord
powering its electrical intelligence,

the weather cranks north
an inch a day to new understandings,
how to keep the fallacy
that music or humans might do anything,

how to lift the clouds' tenor
into infallibility, how
his horn feels, gutted by the rag
in the hatchback's nest.

AIRLESS WONDER

As the glass cake cover descends
my breath ups the humidity. Outside, the burro
continues his circles, spirographing his life away
and the fishermen, up to their waists, advance

without ceremony into the profuse
medium of medium. The music tries to lead
and my leash catches short. My cake glass
is made of clear lead and loss. The worry machine

clocks its twenty-four-hour shift. Its workers,
their caps of kestrel feathers, their hands free
to lock my throat. Work will set you free,
whispers the grass and the broken speakers

and the metal of the constantly conversing
swings. I look for a drinking straw
somewhere discarded, with the leftover
breath of a person not unhappy,

a person whom chest-high waves do not deter
from calmly lowering a net
into the opaque water, scooping out
the silver, slight fish. To reach without seeing.

To be a diver in the dark. To have
no glass. The clear air and the wet turmoil
of their forearms. They do not startle.
The water hits their lips, the net is heavy, the silver

close. Little carp with their pale-rose bellies
below the concrete walkway, the ardent damp.
One turns in the water. I lift the glass:
disaster. I keep the glass: disaster.

THE THIRTEEN-YEAR SLEEP

In the sideways moving sea
of Progreso, we admitted
to fear of everything. If I dream

of you again my skin may disappear,
I will be pure air, mixing
with the Belarus snow, the bay

where my parents fought their little fights,
the ancient hillocked civilizations of polished shards.
When your letters arrive the world

opens at its shellfish fracture
where all the sea meets all the shore.
The imprecision of sound becomes

the Theme Time Radio Hour of loneliness.
Saint Francis' wooden arm loses
another chunk to the beasts. The metalworker

reduces shard after shard to dust,
melts it down, begins again. The sheets
in the dryer have buttons. Buttons

that throw themselves against the metal drum
in an unsyncopated admission. Am I leaf or
flower? Do I change my own colour?

The art of losing is the art
of multiple feelings, colliding
like blood cells in their race from one

low-pressure wall to another.
Multiple feelings are like wanderlust.
They're not satisfied cleaning a car.

They slam the door, run to the neighbour,
launch and mate in mid-air, a touch
and it's done, only to fall to pieces

as when the beetles arrive, breaking
their own wings off their own bodies
then walking into the earth. Would you like

a new country? In every one
mine were slew. In Russia
it was an orthodoxy; in America,

a wife; in Canada, an academic; I gift you
six cypresses, their skirts dying, their heads aimed
to the possibility of an ahistorical star.

ARDENT

My father said, *I'd do it all again*, all the sorrow and delight,

and I was hovering somehow above the green kitchen
and the hide chair, the chain-link and the women calling

for their children as the boy kicked the ball
the wrong way on purpose. I'm wearing three layers of feeling.

The first is willow green, innermost, brushing my skin
like nettles. I love its electric. The second is plasma,

newly discovered like the giant pasta tubes
that surround the earth, and in the third

all but the most ardent extras have gone home. Any day
now I shall be released to the Bangladesh runway,

its burnt out plane a little hulk from a different dimension,
a researcher of longing, no one selling Heineken

from a cooler in its unlit aisles, no one with a line to God.

I had my father over the summer I was in the crater.

His wife was burying her father
by the great lake no one swims in. I jerked through rooms

that had held a ridiculous marriage. He watched me drink,
sitting below the swallow's nest and the dark firs.

I came out to open air for the first night in months, drawing
our history in my book, eating what he had brought,

or he ate it, at any rate. Our talk was a silliness like kissing
while laughing—he still wanted me to think he was cool.

Death had been a balm. I looked back
to the couch I'd made bed, the interior of the dark,

from the sharp, sweet surprise of arbutus air. We
were taken in by weightlessness, by Solstice Hill.

Since then I try to slow down
but I can't. I try to slow it down but I can't.

Ana came over this morning.
She never phones, she just comes.
We drank coffee. I was trying

not to be nervous, to speak more
into the microphone of translation.
Then she was crying, about her son,

who feels guilty not earning enough
before his first baby comes. His wife Isa
is eighteen and has skin like gold

dust. The echo in transmission
caught up to itself as she wiped at her eyes.
I forgot to offer a tissue. I watched as the minute

hand ratcheted our relationship
back to first words. Don't cry,
I thought. I took a breath and ate the air

that is someone else's country.
Who was the person who thought
up being drawn and quartered?

What was it like outside? What happened
that morning? It wasn't
until a week in I realized the hours

in the kitchen's bird clock weren't matched
to their songs. Northern oriole was singing
white-throated sparrow's song. Now

I'm speaking with a clock in my lap,
unsure how to proceed. It seems wise
to defuse the object that steals

by reducing its voice. But sometimes a voice
is a sob. She asked for tissues,
then we went shopping.

I bought her flan, she bought me bread,
we ate croissants, drank milk. She told me
more stories of the people on our street.

Tu suegro, glancing to see how I'd take it,
kicked three of his sons out of their houses.
She didn't like the croissant but saved

the worst for last and then ate it all.
Before she left she did all the dishes.
When she walks it's like she's gliding.

AUTOMATIC PILOT

My brain's main man picks off
any new growth from
its badly cut limbs, stores the

wretchedness in the crater. I would
blame it on him, but it's me
who suspects you'd steal coins we're saving

for the next game of pool. He brings out
his rototiller, churning through air like a lake
weed machine. When he's around too long you

become pieces, your hand or an
emotion diced into chimichurri while
racking up the next game. O

my little rototilling mascot, won't you
ever get fed up? My cup threateneth not
to run over. In my sky throne, the rainstorm

I plow through gives way to children
careening from the rubble of cars,
the damp sweet smell of the world as it saunters

out from its secret tree.
I am the operator of those incessant
tappings you hear at night while trying

to sleep the sleep before the interview.

I am the interviewer. Please believe me.

My galaxy became sad. I, too, wanted to be yours.

GEODES

Up in my starship, I realize
all the eyes are away shopping
at Walmart. I operate the sky paddles,

stop and pick you up. We go for a joyride.
The hummingbird mascots, radio collars
operational, show us their cloud pictures.

My fingers leave the controls, your thin
body unfolds itself like a nebula
as we drift through the galleries

of each galaxy unseen. Each solar system
is up and running. In some the baubles
shine, in others, a stampede of dust

overtakes us, veers us toward a green
thunder that sounds
of our long-ago rains. Outside the bubble

of the skylight the occasional junk ship
hawks spectacular mangoes and packets
of glowing seeds. It's from you I learn

nowhere is my home. We are flying
through the star pods, the thick glass
and metal flukes enduring the blows.

The crystals inside us begin
to magnify, to reach and fuse.
In ten thousand years they'll display us

in the latest incarnation
of a museum—examples
of how an insignificant shell

can house, sealed from the world,
an inner chamber
of intricate light, of arc, of gold.

VOYEUR

We are wheeling through life
as though in a grocery cart.
Aisle after aisle after aisle goes
by, flavour and promise, but

we are too small to reach.
The good is beyond our grasp.
But we look.
We stare in awe

at the kaleidoscopes of taste.
Meanwhile, the little trees
soak up their summer rains.
The lake rises, branches burst

forth in a tearing that is the person
we love hurting us the first time.
It's why as runners we stride so close
to pass. We want to be closer,

always closer,
so loping, we gift
sweat and breath.
Bumping along the path, casters

long gone, keys
playing themselves,
a piano singing a waltz
trails like a dog.

We can look. We can look—
something will sing for us.
We can look.
Love will break us

but our work,
cacophonous, continuous,
will lift us like gems
into the jeweller's silent eye.

A SHADOW NO MATTER HOW IT TRIES CANNOT TURN TO GOLD

Watching the *son istmeño* singers
    Kim calls a choir
I remember the rows

of dolls my teacher
    collected
from around the world

displayed in her tiny studio
    a converted garage
in glass cases above the piano

grey lace on the top board
    hundreds
of tiny eyes staring out

in their finery
    the flamenco red
of the Spaniard the wimple

of the English nurse
    the Mexican ruffles
like those on stage now

at her Christmas recitals
    pizzas
we ate on her floor

the sky pieces
    emerging as each student
touched the keys

later someone
    built an addition
on her tiny house and the garage

is a garage again but the whistles
    the voices
the keys the whisper of air

moved through the cabinet
    kept me
from committing crimes

I have been convicted of
    or I may have
in those moments felt

as her finger punched the correct key
    the manifestation
of all my electric anger

running like a lamp's current
    through my hands
I waited once for her

to give me one
    she must have
ordered them as she never travelled

but she didn't and I was eight
    and livid
her piano too loud

fourteen years leaning back
    when I was doing well
forward to point or pound

when I faltered
    her husband
on an oxygen tank and then not there

my father began writing cheques
    for twice her rate
each week a little fight

their eyes stare now
    from another collector's
shelf or a Saint Vincent de Paul's

I'm going to
    throw this clay
cup   to the floor

I'm going to   ask for my love

    and be naked

    when he arrives   let him
                                    come and come inside me

while   rain
                           inundates
our room   I'm going to

pull the women in their white lace
     off the stage
and hurt them

TEN THOUSAND CONCORDANCES AND ONE THOUSAND ILLUSTRATIONS

Is it because we know it will end?
Is it because I flaunt it that I need it?
Do you want more?

Will you be taken in the night, walking
under jasmine, the cupola, the *bóveda*?
Is the river of rainwater dark? Will our nights

prevent the vehicle's leer? There is a sinkhole
in our barrio, it tails your steps.
It shakes down your friends, whispers up

the *falcones*, trembles images
that should be good and clear. We are not good.
No one likes this much joy. Let the hunt begin.

Let the worker in Michoacán lever the gates
open late at night, shunt the water and its martial
lilies into the engorging lake. It thunders

over the spillway, rakes the metal rivets, sheens
the once-river mud of the sluice, the midnight
channel. It is your family dying on the one blank curve

of highway where the train tracks cross
and the train that was not supposed to cross
at that moment was paid to cross

at that moment. The money appeared
on the Minister's desk like a caress. Let the water
take you away. The dam doors clamp like a jaw.

The lilies star onto the lake. By dawn
implanted in the shallows,
or adrift like cut-up sentences—*Te amaba*...

Eras...   *Deberías*...   *Hicieron*...
In the calm green of shallows they catch on fences
dug and strung over mud flats in times of drought.

OPEN WHEN ALONE

Hello, old feeling.
It's not been long enough.

Access to the central holding
facility of joy has been curtailed

for all those not in a pool
or cutting pine

with an antiquated saw. *Pendejo*,
call the boys, while a love song

croons, its accordionist high
on playing the straight man. Again

and again, the flicker into new
territory, then out

to alight like Napoleon the hummingbird
on the chain-link, just inside

the zone of ownership.
Every time he flies past he takes

another handful of dust off
my body. By tomorrow, just

the sheen of mechanicality,
like how a swimming pool changes

from turquoise to white smear
when used as it should. Little

voice, you're like those coloured
flags planted atop the next

to furthest jungled hill. It will
never be easy, say your flickering

oyster-shell forms. You'll never get out of this alive.
Another love song concurs. *And*

I'm hungry and cold, adds the singer,
her armies all

burned at the edge of the city.
Give me the pass, I whisper

to the little voice. You can
have my first-born, my money,

the almond croissant I'm eating by pieces
to pretend I'm not eating

the whole thing. You can
have the North's lotus-eaters

the dark firs and my moon
rising with Pluto, poor Pluto,

in one of twelve houses, which was told to me
this morning but because I

am without any earth apparently
leaves my head immediately.

I see a bare arm gleam
at the pool's edge and think I

might just believe in Innisfree,
in the guillotine operator

shading his eyes, seeing his wife,
hooking the leather strap to hold the

metal blade before stepping off the wood
platform through the crowd.

I am tired and volcanic. I would never
have made a good Penelope.

I'd have taken the suitors one
by one on the infinite cushions

of the daybed with its view
of the sea, then had them

brutalized by dogs. One of the boys
paddles to the concrete

edge of the water, levers out
to his waist, then falls back in,

he does this again and again
and it is the most pleasurable

thing in the world,
obviously, to use

himself between mediums
like this to be

briefly, perfectly,
both latch and key.

EL DICTADOR

Sometimes I think he is all of us.
Sitting on the tailgates of our cars

in the tumbling light, staring out
at the weighted storm that will not

pass overhead but slant south
missing us, a lodestone of the berry farms,

pine forests, the volcano that coughs.
Playing each track as a balm.

There was *that moment,*
sang Shirley Horn, *when my heart,*

sitting beside the back tire, beat
wildly against its instrument case. When

the white bird picked its way closer
and ate all our pain. He puts his lips

together, trying to look elsewhere.
The lake turns to river and begins

to slick by. Leaning back, he watches
things of wood and wing, things of praise

and shame, the larger skiffs
and the smaller tempests. Every night

the spark of speakers, holding
his hand out, filling it, handing us

a world broken by Milanés
into faultless rafts. Are you

ready to go any time? he asks.
Are you ready to go?

MIRACULOUS FAILURE

I started reading your books in hopes
of a secret message in the lines.

I wanted a little,
a cloud pulley, fellow traveller operating

delicate lines like gossamer.
There was nothing like that poetry.

Occasionally, things were amusing—
the Virgin of Guadalupe's image

as a vagina, when your protagonist
sleeps with his one lover, before

he becomes a simulacrum. Nothing
like the poetry to which we turned

with its ghosts and the
black crater identical to mine.

Like the peeling scroll
of this table I followed it

until it too ate me and spit me
into the brightness that waters.

The scroll just keeps going,
unrolling

until I turn gold, transferred
to skin like a Delhi temple.

I won't shake it off.
There's nothing left of you.

There was nothing like our poetry
always bone blue, always talking to me.

FITZGERALD

I leave alone and paddle
into the sun from Loon Bay's shade.

The lake is a child's skin. The sun
a burning hand. Cliffs

holding lodgepoles, kingfishers.
A woman suns herself on the small island,

jumps in. No engine no voice.
Lake the colour of first sex in a year.

Brief, dark, bottomless, without generosity.
It is freedom from thought. I am in the canoe

and cannot see the canoe's red.
I am the girl on shore feeling water

take over my shoulder blades.
I am my dog on shore, swimming out,

giving up, turning back. I am the canoe,
revolving an island of wind.

I am the granite cliff and the sex hits me
like a perfect paragraph of Fitzgerald's.

I want Fitzgerald islands and
Fitzgerald sex, Fitzgerald meals

under a dozen stars, alone, the glow
of a green light across the bay.

CHESTERMAN

I am a mole at its burrow's edge, fixed by
the grey sun. All day, twelve-foot ten-second sea,
southwest twenty-five knots. My back to the salal

it's growing sandier and sandier. With a boom
another roller lands, the horizon stands up, sits down,
a Parkinsonian but delighted crowd.

A boy jumps like a fox in the dusk air.
I consider breaking out the officially-happy-again card.
Decide to delay. Crossover clouds

smother the sunset; my dog on the wide beach
is a pool of mercury on the deck of a ship at anchor
in a casually protected harbour.

Walking, we pass the maintenance man, readying
Frank Island's love cabins with Presto logs
and a cooler of champagne. The metal wheels

of his cart drag; he sighs. The sea subsides,
surfers festoon it, metal filings to a magnet,
their dogs motionless on shore. Sometimes

the mind is a hopper and it doesn't bother itself.
Everything, even the cart's imperfect tracks,
is paradise, silvered highballs, white noise,

no storm moving soundlessly in,
and the surfers like rickshaw drivers
whose feet never touch ground.

LOVE

It is likely that my father and my dog
will die the same year. They are both

in their retirement. They complain.
They smile. They look as if

they wish there were something
more they could do for me.

The universe of tinnitus presses in
like the swell of a drama.

I'm not mad, I say to my ex-love.
I'm not going to be mad anymore.

I'm lying in this bed. My father is
by the sea, worrying. My dog,

her back to me, hangs her muzzle
off the edge, out into the space

between comfort
and the hundred-year-old floor.

She sighs when I touch her
and does not move closer.

GRACE

This little insect,
a miniature cricket,

    thread legs,
    body of an angular banana,

navigates the folds
of the Bashō palm in fits

and starts. Every
morning in his life,

    as the storms lift,
    then drop, he stops

he has *anhelo*, he gambols, he has *querencia*, he bows.

CURTAIN

The wind knocks the lakeside tansy and sorrel down.
We need not fall apart to feel the feeling.

The stems rise again in the intake between gusts.
Maybe we have the blue cloak of translation, a dog

shepherding our sounds. Maybe
someone plays for us while we sprawl

on a stone floor in night's blue. Maybe it is our story,
named what we could have been

had the poles been reversed, the losers
the victorious, the pen the page. Under the scroll

of water the hyacinths rise and fall as new land.
The shore takes them up as corsages,

pins its own breast. Maybe we will be saved by loss,
the green bouquets held by force

while the shore climbs its stepladder.
The stepladder's feet are

unsteady in sand. The green
nudges a world briefly lithe and learned.

It flickers in our minds, flames itself
out, carbon from coal,

rising as it falls.

LEVITATION

I begin the rainy season's daily
deconstruction, put on the guise
of a cantankerous woman. All I ever wanted
was the same table and chair
in a hundred places around the world.
And someone at night to talk to. Like you.

Without my nest I wander to the water
where wind is gleaning hills, making
light into mantles. A couple
I imagine as French unwrap a bottle of wine,
set glasses on their bench. He wears
dark glasses and a chocolate-bar moustache.
The soccer game beyond them has

no out-of-bounds lines. The boys
chase the ball across the path and off
the walkway and sometimes they play
in the air above the blossoming sand.

ACKNOWLEDGEMENTS

Some of these poems appeared previously in the following journals and anthologies: *Canadian Literature, Sweet Water: Poems for the Watersheds, El Ojo del Lago, Geopoetics in Practice, Ravel.* Thank you to the editors, collaborators and publishers of these publications, and to the Comox Valley Art Gallery for a collaborative residency and creation grant. An early version of this collection appears as a chapter in my doctoral dissertation, *Lyric Geography: Geopoetics, Practice, and Place.* I am also grateful for support from the Canada Council for the Arts and Access Copyright Foundation.

These poems owe a debt to Matthew Zapruder for his beautiful work on hard feelings. Thank you also to Jan Zwicky and Argel Corpus for their work, and for providing notes to introduce this book.

This book was written predominantly while I was living in Jalisco, México, and the country's colours, sounds, people, complicatedness and beauty deserve all the credit. Many helped the project along, providing sustenance of all kinds: laughter, food, drink, language, dwellings, inspiration, love. Thank you especially to Jeanne Campos, who as we walked up the cobblestones on our first meeting, said (laughing), "Oh you're an artist, too? Well, we're both doomed, then!" To Bob and Sandy Pierson for further laughter. To Anna, Magda, Hortencia, Marlene, Marika and their families, not just for feeding me, but for inviting me in.

Gratitude and love to Christian Fink-Jensen for his editing and design help (and for every other kind of love) and to Sam and Kieran Fink-Jensen.

This book is for Maximino Chavarría Mendoza. And with gratitude for Antonio Andrade, El Dictador, and for (too little) time with Andrés Acosta. *Que soy pájaro libre, y que estoy ligada por ti.*

ABOUT THE AUTHOR

Maleea Acker lives in unceded Esquimalt, Songhees and W̱SÁNEĆ territories on Vancouver Island. She is the author of two previous poetry collections, *The Reflecting Pool* (Pedlar Press, 2009) and *Air-Proof Green* (Pedlar Press, 2012), as well as a non-fiction book, *Gardens Aflame: Garry Oak Meadows of BC's South Coast* (New Star Books, 2012). She has lived, worked and been an arts fellow in Canada, the US, Spain and Mexico. Acker holds a PhD in geography and teaches geography, Canadian studies and literature at the University of Victoria, Camosun College and Thompson Rivers University.